Jean Gaume

Suema, the Little Africa Slave

Jean Gaume

Suema, the Little Africa Slave

ISBN/EAN: 9783744724906

Printed in Europe, USA, Canada, Australia, Japan

Cover: Foto ©ninafisch / pixelio.de

More available books at **www.hansebooks.com**

Suema

OR

The Little African Slave:

A TALE OF OUR OWN TIMES,

FROM THE FRENCH OF

MGR. GAUME,

Sold for the Redemption of Negro Children in the Catholic Mission of Zanzibar.

White man, buy me, that I may have something to eat.
My child, I would buy you, but I have no money.

Page xiv.

DUBLIN:
W. B. KELLY, 8 GRAFTON STREET.
1871.

Contents.

	PAGE.
INTRODUCTION.	
I. Zanzibar	v.
II. The Catholic Mission	ix.
III. The Missionary among the Negroes	xiii.
IV. Charity must triumph	xxi.
DEDICATION.	1
SUEMA.	
Chapter I. The Slave Trade	9
II. Suema's Country	19
III. Strange and Superstitious Customs	23
IV. Suema's Childhood	27
V. Suema's Father killed by a Lion	32

SUEMA.

	PAGE
CHAPTER VI. Famine	37
VII. Misfortune still	40
VIII. Journey in the Desert	45
IX. Filial Love	48
X. Maternal Love	53
XI. The Last Separation	57
XII. The Voyage	61
XIII. Buried Alive	64
XIV. Disinterred again	68
XV. Suema's Confession	71
XVI. Suema's Heroism	75

INTRODUCTION.

I.

ZANZIBAR.

FROM the remotest antiquity the Eastern coast of Africa has been frequented by Arab and Indian merchants. The learned recognize in that country the Ophir of which the Bible speaks, where it mentions the Phœnicean ships sent by Solomon in quest of ivory and gold. Towards the year A.D. 1010, a colony of Shiraz under the leadership of Ali, son of a king of that country, built the city of Quiola, which afterwards became the capital of a great kingdom.

In the sixteenth century the Portuguese made themselves masters of this country, but were contented with making it acknowledge the sovereignty of their king. They were, however, soon driven out by the Iman Muscat, who became master of the whole coast from Cape Guardafui to Cape Delgado.

On the death of Said Ben Sultan in 1855, the Imanate of Muscat was divided into two independent kingdoms, that of Muscat under the rule of Toveny, and that of Zanzibar governed by the intelligent and distinguished prince who actually reigns, the Said Meggid.

"Our mission," writes Father Horner, "includes all the States of the Sultan of Zanzibar, that is to say, one thousand five hundred miles of coast. The authority of the Sultan is represented by military governors called tehmators who are appointed to the principal offices of State. The feudal element prevails in the actual government, which is kindly disposed, and gives unbounded liberty to all religions.

"The island of Zanzibar enjoys a more temperate climate than one would imagine from its geographical position. Lying close to the continent, it is cooled by land and sea-breezes. The rainy season lasts forty days; and in the great heats, the night-dews replace the rains. The island is remarkable for its fertility; enormous mangroves, cocoa-nut trees, spice-trees, etc., give it the appearance of an enormous forest surrounded by a border of flower-knots.

"The town of Zanzibar, capital of the island is, from the importance of its trade, also capital of the whole east coast of Africa. It contains a population of 80,000 souls; the entire island may have about 380,000. The roadstead of Zanzibar, which is excellent, gives an anchorage every year to 60 large ships and about 12,000 boutres,* bringing the produce of the soil or the manufactures of the neighbouring countries from Madagascar and Mozambique to Delgado, and even to the end of the Persian Gulf.

"There are four consuls in Zanzibar, representing England, France, Prussia and the United States; yet there is nothing attractive in it, except the unbounded liberty you enjoy. The Indians have their processions with wooden horses in the streets of the town. We perform our funeral ceremonies with the hymns of the Church, and far from offending us in our religious ceremonies, the Arabs respectfully stand up as we pass. It would be difficult for you to have an exact notion of the tranquility and esteem which Europeans enjoy here. I have gone over the whole island unarmed, and everywhere I met the most generous hospitality.

"What astonishes the natives beyond expression,

---

* Small Arabian barks.

is to see the whites, whom they look on almost as gods, employing themselves about the sick and giving them medicines. The disinterestedness of the Missioners strikes them above all: 'How is it possible,' they say, 'these whites, such great men, so powerful, should deign to help us in our sickness? The whites,' they continue 'are so much more intelligent than we, their religion therefore must be much better than ours, because they know better how to choose.'"

II.

THE CATHOLIC MISSION.

WE are sure that the little story of Suema will be read with increased interest, when we have heard from the lips of the Venerable Superior of the Mission the state of Catholicity, its trials and its hopes in the far off country, where our young heroine's lot is cast.

"Six years ago" he tells us "the mission of Zanzibar was confided to me: at that time it consisted of fourteen orphans. Now thanks to the alms of European Catholics, our children amount to sixty-five. The interior of Africa is also open to us. Several tribes who have visited us wish to see us established among them. With a view to make the work lasting, we are building a house to form native priests and catechists, who will go and regenerate their poor brethren in the interior.

"The Sultan, who has been always kind to us, gave us a grant of excellent land, nearly five miles in circumference, at Bagamoyo. Here I have established the children destined for agricultural labour. During the nine months the boys have been on the coast, there has been no death or even serious sickness amongst them. They spend the time, which is not devoted to religious instruction and elementary education, in clearing the land and digging the soil. This patriarchal life suits the little blacks perfectly, and brings them naturally to Christian civilization.

"The land granted to us is a forest of brushwood. The clearing of it, our first occupation, will be a costly affair, but, at the end of a few years, the property will be able to furnish means to found Missions in the interior of the continent. The place chosen for our establishment is one of the healthiest on the whole coast. It is on an elevated spot, whence there is a boundless view of the Indian Ocean, and our solitude is within ten minutes' walk of the village of Bagamoyo. We erect our buildings of loam, and cover them with reeds. It is troublesome enough to raise those edifices, as it is the savages, arrived from the interior with the Arab caravans, whom we have to employ, and they have not the least idea of the art of building.

"We have already received some of them, who show themselves very anxious to become acquainted with our holy religion. These good Nyamouezis receive threepence halfpenny a day. When we cannot give them any employment, for want of money, it is pitiable to see the poor people. They come to us saying, 'Give us work, we are sick with hunger.' And can you guess how they feed themselves when they cannot earn? They go into the forest, where they break off the leaves from the trees and eat them, and as hunger and want make them ingenious, they season the ragout with locusts, which they dress with leaves of trees.

"I have introduced to Zanzibar the use of the plough; it has done wonders. I have to act as architect, carpenter, mason, cabinet maker, and in fact jack-of-all-trades. The little house we inhabit is covered with straw; it has one small door and no windows, the usual style in this country. We have therefore to use lights to read by in the middle of the day. The want of air has rendered the place so bad that grass grows all over it. It had been uninhabited for five years, on account of the deaths or diseases it had witnessed, and it has become a perfect nest of insects and filthy animals. At night, our sleep is disturbed by multitudes of rats, which run over our beds; and by enormous ants, which cover us from head to foot; and sometimes by serpents, which come to our pillows to avoid the cold of the night, mosquitoes and other unwelcome guests also come and annoy us. Outside we are scarcely more fortunate—we have sometimes to defend ourselves against wild beasts of all kinds. If by chance we are able to procure a few chickens we are forthwith visited by tigers, jackals, tiger cats, civet cats, hyenas and boa-constrictors, who come in the night and devour everything. The hippopotamus also joins the marauders, and aggravates our miseries by eating the vegetables we planted with so much trouble in our little kitchen-garden.

"I need not dwell on the works we execute under a burning sun, which often gives some of us long and severe fevers, during which we have neither suitable care nor lodging. Privations, fatigue, and illness retard the completion of our permanent house. A large wooden Cross, in the midst of which we inserted a picture of the Sacred Heart pierced with a sword, is placed on its highest point. The symbol of our religion, the symbol of real happiness is seen from afar, and in the midst of the cross the flames of love from the Adorable Heart of Jesus, awaiting the day when we shall be able to raise a sanctuary in its honor. Our chapel in the island is consecrated to St. Joseph, and that at Bagamoyo is dedicated to the Immaculate Heart of Mary.

III.

THE MISSIONARY AMONG THE NEGROES.

"SUCH is Zanzibar as to its climate and our position there. With regard to its moral state the picture alas will have dark shading! We see in it but the natural fruit, the deplorable results of African paganism, which inspired by the father of lies, a murderer from the first, has transformed man into a ferocious beast.

"Not to speak from the testimony of others, I shall cite facts of which I have been ocular witness more than a hundred times. If you wish to know the fruits of paganism, go to the custom-house of Zanzibar, where the poor slaves are landed. I defy the most hardened heart to look at these poor blacks without being moved. They arrive in a state of perfect nudity, they appear starved and just like skeletons. The dull eye, the arms crossed on the breast, almost dying with hunger and thirst, sad and silent, save for the expression of suffering there is nothing human about them.

"From the custom-house, after paying the duty—the tax on a man is the same as that on an ox—they are brought to the slave-market as a vile herd. The purchasers come, each inspects the one he wishes to buy, just as he would a beast of burden at a fair. The auctioneer sets them up, one after the other, to the highest bidder. At such times, I often have come across little children, who summing up all the life left them on their lips thinned by starvation, would say to me with a suppliant look and wan smile,

"'White man, buy me; with you, I shall have something to eat and will be happy.'

"Ah! how my heart bled when I had to reply,

"'My poor child, I would wish to purchase you, but I have no money.'

"What a grief to the Missioner, not to be able to succour so many wretched people, so many souls, to whom, with a little money, he could open the gates of heaven! And to think that for two pounds he could redeem from slavery a child of six or seven years old, and that he has not that sum, which is so often wasted in the world on frivolous and dangerous indulgences."

Among the tiger-hearted dealers, who carry on the traffic in human flesh, none is better known than the Gelaba. His name signifies robber, and his whole industry is confined to the stealing of young children, especially of little girls of four years old and over. As fond of gain as he is cruel, the Gelaba does not shrink from travelling hundreds of leagues into the interior of the country in search of his prey. These heartless wretches, like vultures, hover near the dwellings of the poor negroes, until they find a fitting moment to exercise their rapacity.

At Tybeb, in the heart of central Africa, lived a negro family, one of the wealthiest in the land. Its peace was often troubled by Gelaba, who wished to carry off and sell its daughters, three young girls. But their father always flew to their defence, and so valiant was he, that the robbers were ever obliged to abandon their enterprise. However he soon died and left his wife and children helpless. Every moment the poor mother trembled lest she might see her daughters torn in pieces by ferocious beasts, or what she feared still more, fallen into the hands of Gelaba, who would drag them from her bosom to the slave market. At nightfall, she anxiously gathered her little ones around her and carefully closing every opening in her hut, piled up behind the door all the furniture she possessed, forming with it a kind of rampart. Fortunate in protecting them from the claws of the lion and tiger, she was not equally so in shielding them from the clutches of the Gelaba.

While working in the fields, with her children helping her or amusing themselves on the grass, she had often noticed sinister faces peering at them. Those strangers beckoned to the children to come and follow them, as if they had something to give or say to them in private. At this sight the poor mother's blood would freeze in her veins, and as a hen, who sees the hawk hovering near, she was preparing to quit the lonely country and seek out a place of greater security for herself and children. But one night, while the family was plunged in sleep, the noise of persons overturning the furniture piled up behind the door was suddenly heard. They leap terror-stricken from their beds, but alas—too late! A band of armed Gelaba seize them, force them under the pain of instant death to be silent, so that their cries may not awaken their neighbours, and then bind them hand and foot. The youngest child frightened at this strange scene screamed aloud, and was immediately torn asunder before the eyes of his mother and sisters. The ruffians travel the entire night without stopping, dragging along with them their unfortunate victims. Having reached a spot, where they thought themselves safe from the pursuit of their captives' friends and neighbours, they halted to share their plunder. The mother fell to the lot of one, the daughters were divided among the others, and their separation was eternal.

One of these poor children, hardly seven years old, soon fell sick from sorrow, fatigue, privation and ill treatment. Her master to whom she had now become a source of trouble, ordered another slave to climb a tree and tie the little girl up in it hand and foot, and then went his way. She was almost dead when another troop of Gelaba passed the same road. One of them seeing the little girl hanging thought from the motion of her limbs and the fearful moaning to which she still gave utterance, that she was not as yet dead. He ascends the tree, looses therefrom his unexpected booty, and tries to recall her to life. The child recovers her senses, the brigand leads her amidst his band, who gibe at this good fortune. After a few hours' march the little girl becomes faint as before. Then the Gelaba thinking that she would soon die, threw her with a kick on the sand, and continued his journey, without even the cold mercy of having her tied up in a tree, to prevent her falling a prey to the tigers.

But providence was watching over the little orphan, a negro, who served as guide to the caravan of a rich merchant, perceiving the unfortunate child, went towards her, took her on his camel, and so brought her to the first market, where he sold her as damaged goods for a low sum. Her health, however, improving, she was frequently sold and resold, till at length the Venerable Father Oliviere found her exposed in the slave market of Alexandria. He purchased her and brought her to Europe, where, having become heroically Christian, she died in the odour of sanctity, having hardly attained her sixteenth year.

Another child of the desert, saved too by the holy priest whom we have just named, tells us in her own simple language another sad tale,—

"My mother was very beautiful, but black. She had very many servants. My papa had always nice clothes, not like the Turks, but like the Arabs. I was their only child. They let me play by myself in the garden, which was closed by a narrow gate, so that the Gelaba might not get in.

"One day, while I was playing there with a lot of little pebbles, I heard some one walking behind me, when I turned round I saw a Gelaba with a long knife in his hand, and carrying on his shoulders a bag all covered with blood. I stood up, and was running away crying, but this man caught me by the hand and said, 'if you cry out, I'll cut off your head and put it in my sack.' I withheld my tears, in order that I might not be put in that awful bag, but my heart beat so quickly that I could hardly breathe, and the Gelaba, having taken me in his arms, began to run. When we were far from home he put me down, and holding me by the hand, he ran so quickly, that I was no longer able to follow. I could not take longer steps, for my legs were very little, and blood streamed from my feet all torn with thorns.

"Then the terrible Gelaba, finding I could go no farther, took me in his arms and carried me to his house. His wife, seeing me so very small, took me on her knee. She used a large thorn to draw out the smaller ones from my feet, and then gave me some bread. A few days afterwards the Gelaba set out from home, and tying me with some young negroes, whom he had also stolen, he threw us all on the back of a camel. We remained there very long going on day and night, and once the cord that held us broke, and we were all thrown to the ground, then the driver heaped kicks and blows on us until we had climbed up again.*"

There is hardly anything more sadly true than this young child's story. During ages, such scenes are constantly being enacted in the land of Cham.

What will put an end to them? One thing alone, the conversion to Catholicity of this unfortunate race. But their evangelization requires three conditions:—

Prayers:—Our nuns established in the different parts of Africa offer them abundantly and with tears.

Sweat and blood:—Our missionaries shed them in torrents.

Money:—It is for the young Christians of Europe to furnish their sisters' ransom.

"*Do unto others as ye would have done unto yourselves.*"

---

* *Fleurs du désert* p. 14.

IV.

CHARITY MUST TRIUMPH.

"I think it would be almost impossible to give you any idea of the horrors practised among the Vazaramos, five leagues away from our residence. They do not eat each other like the Vadoes, but they are imbued with such frightful superstitions that they murder their twin children or throw them to wild beasts. If a child be born on a Sunday or at the full moon, it is considered unlucky, and is deemed a sufficient reason for dispatching it. If a baby appear weak or deformed, the mother says "it is good for nothing," and either kills it or gives it to the wild beasts. Children when growing up are often the victims of horrid supertitions, and considered worthless if they grind their teeth. O love of Jesus Christ! What miseries, what atrocities are to be met with where Thou art not known!

"Sometimes mothers here are induced to sell their children for two or three shillings, instead of killing them. I saw a little boy of five months old who had been sold for thirteen pence. The poor child was indeed to be pitied. The man who had bought him to make him his slave gave him nothing to eat but mangoes—a fruit something like a pear. I hope to establish a crèche at Bagamoyo. In the opinion of persons competent to judge of such matters, we might buy hundreds of children every year and save their lives and their souls.

"I believe we shall have to pay four shillings a child, because everything is dearer to the whites than to the blacks. I therefore make the greatest exertions to finish the buildings destined for agricultural labour at Bagamoyo. One of these I intend for an infant asylum, where the poor children of the Vazaramos shall be cared for, those so wantonly sacrificed to the demon by the savage superstition of their parents. This will be a tedious affair, but a work beautiful in itself, and suitable to attract the sympathies of good and pious children in Catholic Europe. Little children will be no longer slaughtered, when it is known they can be disposed of advantageously: they will one day become the intercessors for those European children, who, thanks to a little money, shall have saved the life of the body, and, a thousand times more precious, the life of the soul for these poor orphans.

"Oh! how sad it is to live in a country where the mother kills the fruit of her womb! How heartrending, above all to the Missioner, to be unable to remedy as quickly as he would wish so much misery and misfortune!

"O charity of Jesus Christ, when wilt thou come to put an end to such atrocities? Oftentimes my soul is oppressed with grief, to think these poor mothers do not know what it is to caress their children; they more frequently murder or sell them.

"'Blessed is he that understandeth concerning the needy and the poor; the Lord will deliver him in the evil day.' 'Mothers of families reading these lines will say as they look on their beloved children :—' Is it possible that mothers can strangle their babes and throw them to wild beasts? Ought I not try and bring down God's blessing on my own children by doing what I can to diminish the number of such horrors?'

"The greater part of the help we receive for redeeming slaves comes from the associates of the Sacred Heart. In Trinidad the pupils of the Sisters of St. Joseph, at Strasbourg the Sisters of Providence, vie with each other in zeal for the redemption of little negro children, condemned by their parents to the hardest slavery. When I was travelling in Alsace, in 1867, I preached in the Cathedral of Thann about the misery of the slave children, who are sold in the market of Zanzibar. The people no sooner heard that a boy could be bought for one pound, and a girl for one pound fifteen shillings, than they hastened to contribute to the purchase of those poor slaves. Among these persons were two factory girls. One brought me four pounds; her appearance made me guess that her generosity was far beyond her means, and some information that I gathered about her, proved that this sum was the result of many years' hard saving. I had great difficulty in making her take back a part, in order to have something to fall back on. Another workwoman, who was habitually in want herself, brought me one pound fifteen shillings, that I might buy a little girl, and I could not induce her to take back any of it.

" The good Sultan of Zanzibar is one of the best and noblest men that I know, and he has been one of our first benefactors. He has just sent me a note in the following terms:—'A gift of seven hundred and fifty francs for the Fathers of the Catholic Mission to redeem children.' Is not this magnificent from a Mahometan Sultan. May we not hope after that? What a stimulus to the zeal of Catholic hearts?

DEDICATION.

I.

Dear Children,

When very little, you, perhaps, like many others, imagined that the horizon of your native land was the world's farthest limit. But this was an error of short duration.

There is another, however, somewhat similar, which lasts for a longer period. Born in the bosom of Christian civilization, you have believed, many of you perhaps still believe, that all parts of the world are like Ireland and Europe, illumined by the beneficent light of the Gospel. The tender, anxious cares that are lavished on you, the ease and comfort you enjoy, seem so natural to you, that you think the same blessings are bestowed on every child breathing on the face of the earth.

II.

Such an illusion is creditable to you, but, unfortunately, it is an illusion. The story I present you with has for its object to dispel it. You will learn from it what thousands and thousands of young girls, your sisters in Adam and in Jesus Christ, are to-day at some hundreds of leagues' distance from our shore.

Their lot, so widely different from yours, will, I have no doubt, awaken in you the two noble sentiments with which the Creator has so largely endowed woman's heart—gratitude and compassion.

III.

Nor will these be barren sentiments. On learning that among your sisters you are the privileged ones, you will bless with tenderness that God who is twice your Redeemer, at the same time remembering what is written—"To whom much has been given, from him also much shall be demanded."

You will not squander in selfish pleasures the wealth you have received. That would

DEDICATION. 3

be not only degrading your heart by committing the crime of ingratitude, but, in our days especially, directly opposing the call of Divine Providence.

IV.

This call you may plainly recognize in the wonderful spectacle which we witness for the past forty years. Until then, the charitable zeal of the Catholic maiden was confined to merely local objects. But suddenly the spirit of apostleship has fallen on her. Every day, soaring from the ports of France, clouds of chaste doves go forth alighting on every point of the globe. Neither their natural timidity, nor their frailty, nor affection for home and family, nor the allurements of the world, nor wide oceans, nor unwholesome climes, nor savage peoples can arrest that mysterious impulse, urging them to devote themselves to the redemption of their sisters, as the missionary devotes himself to the redemption of his brethren.

At your age, dear children, you cannot as yet walk in the footsteps of your elders by sharing personally in their glorious apostolate, still you can in some measure help to further it.

v.

Are you at school? Then which of you has not her little pocket-money? Why not share it with the wretched? Instead of having it altogether transformed into sweetmeats and playthings, let part of it become the ransom of some of your little sisters who are still seated 'in the shadow of death.'

With one hand your good angel will enter your offering in the Great Book, that it may with interest be restored to you on that day, when the Sovereign Judge shall balance the accounts of each one of us in presence of the assembled nations; while with the other he will make your young heart feel how sweet it is to do good.

vi.

Have you left school? Then whatever be your condition, work-woman or heiress, the means of becoming an apostle are in your hands. Will you allow me to point out to you—not three of them, not even two, but a single one—*kill the leech* that is called *luxury*, and it will turn out for you the hen of the golden eggs.

If you look with an eye of faith, or even of simple reason, at the objects, vain or trifling, not to say sensual, which are so plentiful in your room, on your mantelpiece, on your toilette table. If you even examine yourself from head to foot, what handsome savings for the apostleship you might lay up, without prejudice to good taste.

VII.

And even in indispensable things, why not imitate that admirable companion of yours who said to us—" When Mamma buys any thing for me, I pray her to choose always what is simplest, that I may have something more to help my little sisters of Africa and Oceanica."

But if with all this you are not rich, you have still a last resource.

I know not if under heaven there be a

power so irresistible as that of a gentle and modest young girl, pleading among her friends and the members of her family the cause of the poor, and where are the poor like those of whom I speak?

VIII.

Before making them known to you, I have a word or two of explanation to offer.

In writing those pages, my object is to interest you in a work which I think should be altogether your own. I mean the redemption of the young girls of Eastern Africa.

This work is different from that of the Holy Childhood, whose aim is to save from death the new-born babes sold or abandoned by their mothers, especially in China.

Your work is the deliverance of children older, and thus, if possible, more miserable, because conscious of their lot. In the slave-markets of African towns, very little children are rarely exposed for sale.

The reason is, that this horrible trade is generally supplied with blacks brought from distant countries, and those little creatures could not be carried so far for months, through deserts, and under a burning tropical sun. Besides, their sale would not defray the expenses of their carriage.

It is but right that I should explain to you the meaning of the words prefixed to this little work—'*Do good.*'

That great friend of the poor, Saint John of God, went through the streets of Grenada, a bag on his back, and a basket in each hand, and instead of saying—'*Give me alms,*' he said—'*My brethren, do good.*'

Admirable words, which gave a name to this holy man's disciples, who are still called in Italy the *Fate ben Fratelli*!

IX.

And I too, dear children, have desired to use this language, so divinely beautiful, because so profoundly true.

Yes, beautiful and true! In giving alms, you ennoble your heart, you place at interest that which you bestow, you draw down on yourselves the dew of heavenly benedictions, and, perhaps, even enkindle the ray of light which will guide you to the knowledge of your vocation; perhaps merit the grace which one day will transport you in the footsteps of so many others, for your sisters' salvation, to the world's farthest extremities, making of you new 'heroines of charity.'

If I pray that it be so, could you wish me to do otherwise?

Suema:

OR,

A Tale of African Life.

CHAPTER I.

THE NEGRO TRAFFIC.

TO understand perfectly the following tale, the reader requires some preliminary notions of African slavery.

We will begin, therefore, by describing the negro trade. By this name is termed the infamous law by which the different nations of the world tear away the wretched inhabitants of Africa from their native soil, either by purchase, or even oftener by force, and then export them to the different parts of America, where they are sold like droves of cattle.

This scourge, which has desolated Africa, degraded Europe, and outraged humanity, began its ravages towards the close of the 15th century. When the Spaniards had discovered the New World, they wished to explore the numerous gold mines of that vast continent. They first condemned the conquered natives to this painful task, but the essay was not successful. Accustomed to live in the open air, and to spend their days in the gentler pursuits of hunting and fishing, the Indians perished by thousands, immured in the bowels of the earth. Their masters then resolved to replace them by negroes, in quest of whom they sailed to the shores of Africa.

As soon as the mines were exhausted the negroes were employed in tilling the land.

Thus were the aboriginal tribes, almost annihilated by bad treatment and forced labour, replaced by the hardy Africans—a race which bore the hardships of slavery without murmuring at their fate, and thus better suited for the purposes of European tyranny.

Such was the unholy origin of the negro traffic—one great crime which arose from another. The principle and end of this infamous traffic are in perfect accordance with the revolting method employed in its execution.

The example of the Spaniards was contagious; for, in a few years, the different nations of Europe were all engaged in the abominable trade.

For many centuries, thousands of vessels known as "slave-ships" might be seen coasting along the African shores, from Senegal to the Cape of Good Hope.

To obtain their cargo of human flesh, force, deception, and the allurements of gains were alternately employed. The examples we have before us are so numerous, that the only difficulty we have is to select.

The following instances, taken at random, will suffice:

Some time ago, the slave merchants of St. Louis, being in need of some negroes, armed secretly a few vessels, apparently destined for mere commercial purposes. They landed at Alebia, a village belonging to the tribe of the Pols. These hospitably received the French, without the slightest mistrust, exchanged their commodities with them, and even provisioned their ships. The day was enlivened by feasts and amusements.

But while the Blacks were reposing after the fatigues of the day, the huts were assailed in the dead of night, without the slightest pretext, and the wretched inhabitants, tied hand and foot, and stunned with blows, were either reduced to slavery, or died, fighting bravely for their liberty.

The survivors were then sent across to the plantations of America, where, weighed down by excessive labours, and by the hardships of slavery, they dragged a weary life, oppressed by the unconsolable misfortune of being separated for ever from their wives, their families, and above all, from their fatherland. When the Europeans themselves did not engage in this nefarious pursuit, the very natives did not scruple to do so for their own profit. Travellers, and even the people who live along the African shores, affirm that the generality of the African civil wars have no other motive than that of obtaining slaves for the negro merchants.

Thence results this sad truth, daily confirmed by experience, that as the demands of the negro merchants increase, the negro wars are multiplied. There are nations, such as the Aspautils, who live by making war on their neighbours to obtain slaves.

Father Labat, a Dominican Missionary, relates that the Bis Sagots, have, as well as several other African nations, a great passion for whiskey. "In order to procure it," he says, "the weaker are sacrificed to the mad thirst of the stronger. As soon as a slave-ship appears, the father sells his children, nay, if a child gets the upper hand over his father and mother, they are at once conducted by him to the ship, where he barters them for whiskey!"

An English governor of St. Louis, to obtain slaves, stirred up the Maures against the Oueli. He supplied them with arms, and the other necessary aids, and in two years the Onabian country was devastated—death and slavery had consumed its population.

Another Englishman, the director of the East India Company, informed the King of Yolof that he was about to receive from Europe a cargo of different articles, to be bartered in exchange for negroes. The King immediately gave chase to his subjects, traversing his towns and villages with an armed band which seized upon all the adults fit for export, who had not fled fast enough on his approach. After capturing three hundred, he gave the director to know that he had some merchandise.

The latter hastened to the King to conclude a bargain. The African monarch received the price of his goods, but he was not satisfied. He coveted other

European articles, which were purposely spread out before him, but he had no more men to give.

These goods were then offered to him on credit by the director for three hundred other negroes, on condition that the King would allow him to go take them with his own troops. But, perhaps fearing some snare, the barbarian refused.

All Southern and Central Africa was laid waste by this scourge. According to the most exact statistics, the number of men and women thus carried away from 1768 to 1827 *increases each year by one hundred and twenty-two thousand*! By this statistic, the number for 58 years will be 7,040,000!

This, however, does not comprise the victims of the innumerable wars which are caused in the pursuit of the trade.

As the negro export trade has now lasted 300 years, and was formerly even more active and general than now-a-day, we are still far below the real number, if we conclude that from the discovery of America the nations of Europe have, without other right but that of being the stronger, reduced to slavery more than *thirty-five millions* of human beings! And they think that God will bless them!

To be torn away from home and family is but the beginning of the slaves misfortune. Laden with chains, and dragged from the interior of Africa, to the place of exportation. He is shut up in a kind of prison till the slave merchant has completed the cargo of human flesh, and when the moment of departure arrives he is conducted, bound with heavy chains, to the floating prison.

"In the ships, where the slaves have most room," says an eye witness, "each occupies little more than a space of five feet in length and one foot in breadth. So situated it is impossible to stand erect, nay, even sometimes to sit down. Lying without clothing on a hard plank, lacerated by the continual motion of the vessel, their bodies are soon covered with dreadful sores, and their limbs torn by the irons which attach them to one another. It is in this wretched state that they make a voyage of from four to five thousand miles. During bad weather, when the sea is rough, and they are obliged to close down the hatches, the sufferings of these poor unfortunates become extreme. By the violent rocking of the ship they are thrown one against the other; they are suffocated by the insupportable heat of the torrid zone, and by the noisome odours arising from so many persons being confined in so limited a space."

In September, 1825, the English Burreu visited near the Old Calabar river—the French vessel 'L'Orphée' having on board seven hundred negroes for transportation to Martinique. The men to the number of 550 were chained two by two, some by the arms, others by the legs, and many by the necks. The odour which proceeded from the place, wherein these unfortunates were heaped pell-mell, was so infectious that the English officer could scarcely support it for an instant. Not, unfrequently, the small-pox, that dreadful scourge, appears among them, and makes frightful ravages. On one occasion more than fifty blacks were found dead in consequence of bad air, but the captain, with the greatest possible indifference, ordered their bodies to be thrown overboard, returned to the coast and supplied their place by new victims. These few instances give but a slight idea of the horrors which take place every day on hundreds of other vessels.

In the petition made in 1826, to obtain the suppression of the slave trade, we read that the captains of slave ships throw each year into the sea more than 1,500 slaves, who have become so crippled from suffering as to be of little value in the market. A great mortality raging among the slaves on board a certain English vessel, the 'Kong,' the captain took the resolution to throw over those most afflicted by the epidemic. The principal pretext he devised for justifying in some way his atrocious intention was the lack of water, though neither the usual quantity given to each sailor, nor even that distributed to the slaves, had been as yet reduced. He then selected 132 of these unfortunates and had them cast into the sea. But Providence, as if wishing to render inexcusable the sacrifice of the remaining victims, sent during three days an abundant rain. Yet, still the captain remorselessly continued in his determination, and ordered the other sick slaves to be precipitated into the deep. Thus was committed in open day a crime of which history presents but few examples.

We should read the life of Blessed Peter Claver, apostle of the blacks, to understand in what state are the poor survivors when they disembark on the shores of America. Once the property of the planter they are treated as animals—the slave is below the beast and has on earth no protector. Constantly subjected to the lash, the law refuses to shield him—his testimony is not received in court. He generally perishes from excess of fatigue or grief, and should he endeavour to escape by flight he is pursued by dogs as if he were a wild beast.

"Often the colonists," says an eye witness, "form themselves into parties of pleasure to give chase to a fugitive negro, with as much unconcern as if he were a wild boar. I knew a lady who procured many a time this amusement for herself and her friends. When the unhappy fugitive, attacked by the dogs, wounded and reduced to the last extremity, implored the compassion of his pursuers, they laughed at his sufferings. Then they cut off his head, which they carried to the rendezvous, in order to receive the prize accorded for the arresting of negroes."

From its very origin the church has not ceased to condemn this abominable traffic. To the anathemas of Alexander III., Leo III., and Paul III., the missionaries joined their protestations, as do all disinterested men, in the question of slavery.

CHAPTER II.

THE COUNTRY OF SUEMA.

THE town of Zanzibar, the capital of the island of the same name, and of a kingdom which extends along the east coast of Africa from Cape Guardafin to Mozambique, having been made the starting point of some of Dr. Livingstone's expeditions, has, of late years, been regarded with no little interest by the scientific world. But it is to the house of the Catholic missions founded at Zanzibar not long ago, by the Fathers of the Congregation of the Holy Ghost and of the Sacred Heart of Mary, that this little story would direct the attention of its readers. There may be seen not less than one hundred and seventy negro children redeemed from slavery by the missionaries in the market place of that town; and there they are brought up with much loving care in the knowledge of the Catholic faith. The boys have their dormitories and workshops in a detached wing of the house, where they are under the especial charge of the brothers of the Congregation, while the girls occupy the rooms near the poor and unpretending chapel. They are taught by the Sisters of Mary from the Isle of Bourbon.

It is a real pleasure to behold the docility, the cheerfulness, the health, and the intelligence of these children—the Christian nursery of Eastern Africa.

Among them is a little girl, scarcely ten years old, who is distinguished by a remarkably tall stature, by the softness of her features, by her humble carriage, and by the naïvety of her language. Her African name is Suema, her Christian name is Madeleine.

When her language became intelligible, her companions, together with the missionaries and nuns, earnestly entreated her to relate to them the events of her life.

With an indescribable air of candour and sincerity, she gave them the following account, which was taken down word for word as it flowed from her lips:—

"I was born in the country of Uamiao; of its extent, of its strength, of its tribes, I have not the slightest knowledge, for I was very small when I left it. All that I know is that it is situated between the kingdoms

Allamnynde and Uamiasse. I have heard that the Naguinado, whose territory is bounded by a kingdom bordering on the ocean, dwell where the sun of the Almnredi rises; that the dominions of the Umiassa extend as far as where the sun sets; and that our nearest neighbours were the Makua and the Uelwauda. My country is extremely beautiful. Its immense plains clothed with a rich herbage, and abounding in precipitous rocks to which the villagers fly in time of war, are traversed by a multitude of streamlets. The rocks are so high that it is thought that they touch the sky. Here and there are large forests abounding not alone in game but also in wild animals. Here, night and morning, the tigers and lions roar incessantly; here, also, numerous herds of elephants graze the verdant foliage. Our fields produce everything that one can wish for. Twice a year did we sow beans, lentils, corn, miarelli, gourds, cucumbers, potatoes, cassada, bredés, wheat, and ignames. The banana grows there like a common forest tree. We sowed rice in the marshy districts, not to eat, for we did not like it, but to obtain in exchange from the Arabian caravans, glass ware, cotton, and salt. In our villages the houses are not connected as here. Between each hut several fields intervene, which are partly cultivated, partly reserved for pasture. This custom is observed in order to preserve the crops from the havoc which would be necessarily caused by monkeys, birds and other animals, as well as to secure the cattle from the wild beasts; the villagers also give this as another reason, that the enemy cannot come by surprise on every one at the same time, nor can they burn all the huts."

CHAPTER III.

STRANGE CUSTOMS AND SUPERSTITIONS.

"OUR cemeteries are formed in the most isolated and remote recesses of the great forests. All were buried in the following manner:—The body was first placed in a little hut composed of the green branches of trees; arrows, bows, javelins, and a shield, were placed beside the corpse, if it was that of a man. If, on the contrary, it was that of a woman, it was surrounded by kettles, ladles, and an immense variety of cooking utensils. The parents of the deceased placed at the feet of their corpse a large plate of flour called rutama, to make porridge. The next morning the parents came to visit the dismal hut. If the meal has disappeared during the night, it is concluded that the person died naturally, and all the neighbours are invited to a great banquet. If, on the contrary, the meal remains untouched, the misfortune is attributed to a witchcraft. In this case the family of the deceased takes up arms for the discovery and punishment of the guilty; and if, as often happens, the dead person belonged to a powerful family, war is immediately kindled in the country. On account of this belief, the origin and reason of which I do not know, whole villages frequently disappear. Such is the position of my country, which, unhappily, does not yet know the true God. But this is not all, as you will see presently. The Zimé dwells in our forests. He is an evil being who eats the people. The most cruel sufferings and diseases are inflicted by him on all who pass near his dwelling, without propitiating him by some offering. It is said that he is a passionate lover of music. Should the person he attacks have the courage to sing or to beat the tambour he immediately begins to dance; his head, his arms, and feet are gradually severed from the body—his eyes leave their sockets, and each member performs its separate dance. At daybreak next morning all the limbs are united and the Zimé disappears."

These absurd and at the same time sanguinary superstitions, of which Suema speaks, prevail over all Africa; and it is almost always the women, and young negresses, who are the chosen victims. In his journey to the sources of the Nile, Capt. Speke describes them as follows:—" While stopping with Rumanika, the King of Karagué, through curiosity I asked him why he sacrificed a cow before the tomb of his father every year, without having any idea of God or of a future life."

"I do not know," he replied with a laugh, "but it seems to me that by doing so I shall obtain better harvests. It is for the same reason that I place before one of the large stones on the mountain a little corn and pombé, though I know well that it can neither eat nor drink. Those who dwell along the coast, indeed all the natives, observe the same customs. Not a single African questions the talismanic powers of magic. If, while leading my troops against the enemy I happened to hear the cry of a fox I would immediately retreat— for this prognostic is said to presage a defeat. But, happily, many other animals, and birds especially, possess a contrary power." In such negroes, and in their customs, we can but too easily recognise the augurers and the omens of antiquity; too plainly can we see that they are as prevalent as in the days of Cicero; truly has it been said that the Devil neither changes nor grows old. With regard to the cruelty of the great enemy of man, who was a "murderer from the beginning," let us again hear what the celebrated traveller says:—

"Having now stopped a considerable time with the King of Ouganda, I have obtained an intimate knowledge of the customs of the place. But will any one believe me when I assert that not one alone, but often three or four unfortunate young women of the harem of Intosa are daily executed. How often have I heard these wretched creatures, while being dragged along by pitiless savages to an ignominous death, make the most heartrending appeals to their persecutors."

Young Christian girls, arm not your hands, but open your hearts in compassion, in order to free your sisters from such a slavery.

CHAPTER IV.

INFANCY OF SUEMA.

DURING the evening recreation Suema continued her story. "My father was very brave, and was considered the best hunter in the country. Throughout the entire year our cottage was well stocked with game and provisions. He was accustomed to sell the tusks of the elephants he had killed to traders, who gave in exchange whatever was required for the support of life. My mother, as well as my elder sisters, were covered with glass beads and chains, they even wore garments which came from abroad. I was also adorned with glass beads, but they were my only clothing. Thus flowed along the fleeting hours of my infancy, unclouded by sorrow or misfortune. In the morning my father, accompanied by his friends, generally set out for the hunting grounds. My mother and sisters hoed the fields while I took care of the sheep and the house.

Some little girls of my own age would often join me, and we sang together like little birds. The days appeared very short to us, and gladly did I hail the evenings which restored my father to the bosom of his family. What a happiness was it for me when I saw my dear papa returning home well pleased with the day's sport and bending under his booty. While I hung upon his neck fondled and caressed, my sisters used to light a fire in the centre of the cottage. My mother then roasted whole sides of venison on the live coals. Immense pots of ugali were then cooked, in addition to the large jars of pombé* that were prepared the evening before. We had always a store of salt laid up to season our food, for, even when the caravans were unprovided with it, my father knew how to procure it. While on his hunting expeditions he had discovered many places where a tall plant grew, the ashes of which have the same qualities as salt. My papa often brought home large bags of these ashes, but to form some idea of the manner in which the salt was prepared, you should have seen us all bustling about at our different tasks. I used to gather wood. One of

---

* A kind of beer.

my sisters fetched water, another washed the ashes, and a third strained off the water through a piece of linen. My mother then superintended the boiling the whole day long, and in the evening we had a few particles of salt. But with us, not every one could have as much salt as he liked. Our neighbours, however, were not so fortunate, for they had no means to procure such luxuries. Their children even considered me so happy, that often when I went to draw water from the river, they would cry out: 'What a happy life Suema leads! She eats meat with salt every day.' I was always pleased with this remark, for it implied a great compliment to my dear father. They often also said: 'See, how smart Suema looks with her braided tresses!' Whenever I heard them speaking thus, I always felt my heart glow with a more ardent love for my mother, for I did not forget that she it was, who had made me look so nice. But, alas! these happy hours passed away too soon."

The heart of the little girl could no longer contain itself, her eyes were filled with tears, and for some time the power of utterance left her. When her emotion had ceased, she added: "Dearest lady, destined henceforth to be a mother to me! Beloved companions, henceforth my sisters, till now I have but showed you the bright side of my life. Soon you will become acquainted with the terrible event which was to be the harbinger of my future misfortunes."

Fearing to fatigue the unhappy child, whose tears now flowed fast at the remembrance of her sufferings, the reverend mother kindly told her to put off the recital of her misfortunes until the following day. The general occupation of young negresses seems to be that of minding sheep. But all are not so happy in their employment or so free from danger as Suema. This we may see from a story told by another young negress who was stolen by a Gelaba, and sold by an accomplice, still more wicked than himself:

"My second master covered me with stripes, and scarcely gave me anything to eat. He sent me to mind his sheep. While thus occupied, I was in a perpetual dread lest I should be eaten up by the wild beasts which roamed through the neighbouring forests. Some of them had very long tails. Others had hands and arms like those of a man. My fears, together with an extreme weakness caused by long fasting, rendered me incapable of attending properly to my charge. On one occasion the Gelaba, seeing that I did not return to his

house with the sheep, came to look for me, and beat me so severely that I was unable to attend any longer to the sheep. He then sold me to another master."
Well may we ask, if men can be found so cruel as to torture in such manner these innocent children? Yet it is so, and such men will always be found as long as Africa remains unregenerated by Christianity.

CHAPTER V.

SUEMA'S FATHER KILLED BY A LION.

A DAY had already passed since Suema discontinued the tale of her childhood, and all now eagerly awaited the moment of her resuming her story. Even Suema herself appeared desirous to lighten the load on her breast by pouring her misfortunes into the hearts of her companions. When asked therefore by the superioress, she continued as follows :—

"My father made arrangements with our neighbours to organize a regular slaughter of all the lesser animals with which Africa abounds. Deep pits, covered with branches and grass, were dug in the localities they most frequented. As soon as this was accomplished, all the families of the hunters united to beat the woods and to go in quest of the game. My father then permitted me, for the first time, to take part in the common chase. I was as happy when setting out as if I were on a pleasure excursion. I did not expect the least danger. Arrived in the forest we formed a somewhat irregular chain, each one remaining several stone throws distant from his neighbour. But as we advanced, all the time shouting as loud as we could, the circle gradually grew narrower and more contracted. While some of the hunters, who were all armed with bows and arrows, ran before the line of the beaters, the others endeavoured to pursue the animals which had adroitly avoided the pits. After a little while we approached the place where the sport of the day really was to begin. We were separated by a very bushy thicket from the chain of beaters. I was walking beside my mother and sisters, while my father was standing a little before us adjusting his arrow on the string. The beating party had just surrounded the skirt of the thicket, when all at once the shouts of the hunters were drowned by the deafening noise of a tremendous roar proceeding from the centre of the thicket. Every one stood petrified, and the noisy cries of the beaters were succeeded by the deepest silence. Then again was heard the sullen roar of the lion, for it was indeed this terrible animal, whose cry was repeated by the echoes of the forest away. I still fancy that I see its glaring eyes, and its bristling mane, as lashing the ground with its tail, it bounded forth from the thicket. The lion approached the hunters who remained motionless for fear. Turning a little aside he suddenly stopped just before us; but, passing my father, he seemed inclined to spring upon my sisters and myself. At the same moment he roared again, still louder than before. Then, my father perceiving the danger which threatened us, and that there was not a moment to lose, at once attacked the angry animal, but his dart and arrows were shot wide of the mark. Then, rushing on, knife in hand, he threw himself on the lion, seizing its flowing mane in one hand, as he raised aloft his hunting knife in the other. I was so terrified by his danger that I could no longer observe what passed. I have a faint recollection of seeing a confused red mass of blood roll along the ground and pass my side, and then disappear in the forest. The struggle had been of so short duration that none of the hunters had time to come to my father's assistance. Then, with piercing cries of heartrung anguish did we throw ourselves already helpless orphans on the earth, stained with the blood of our father, who had proved himself only the too faithful guardian of his fold."

Suema appeared so touched by those painful recollections that the reverend mother thought it better for her to delay the remainder of her story till the following day. "No, mother," replied the little girl, "with your permission, I will now finish my description of that fatal day. Immediately after the disappearance of my father, the hunting party slowly and sorrowfully returned to the village, and the mournful silence of the forest was only broken by sobs and wailings. Night found us still at our solitary post, when the howls of the hyena recalled to my mother's mind that perhaps her youngest child might be in danger from the nightly attacks of that prowling beast. Then my desolate mother arose, but before leaving she made a little hut with the branches of trees, where the ground had been reddened with my father's blood. In it she placed some sagaie together with his quiver and arrows. Then, having left all the provisions on the leaf of a banana at the entrance of the funeral hut, we returned home without once looking behind, for such is the custom of our country in coming from an interment. All my misfortunes date from this fatal day; even that very night was our cottage without light or fire. Nevertheless, we all had to betake ourselves to our ordinary tasks—tasks, however henceforth to be performed in sorrow."

To recruit Suema's strength, the reverend mother delayed the continuation till the following day.

CHAPTER VI.

THE FAMINE.

WHEN the community had again reassembled round her, Suema continued as follows:—

"Oh how unhappy I was then! I did not yet know the consoling truths which have since been taught me. I was ignorant of the great ends of my life, that we were here on the earth to love and serve God, to suffer for him, and by doing so to gain his kingdom. I did not even know how to pray. I was prompted by love of my father and grief at having lost him to hate all creatures. I reproached the sun for shining, the bird for singing, and I cursed my very being, and the joyous tones of my neighbours, instead of cheering, made my breast boil with rage, for they seemed to insult my grief. Such are the torments of those who do not know the true God. Soon after a frightful calamity desolated not only my family but the whole country, on the crops of which fell clouds of locusts. All had disappeared in the short space of three days. While the bark of large trees was gnawed off altogether, the smaller plants fit for food were eaten down to the very root. The country became a desert, and a famine severe as well as general was the result. Those who had salt, subsisted on salted locusts. But since my father's death we were no longer supplied with salt. We lived some time on the goats and poultry which remained in our former well stocked enclosure, but the very beasts themselves not finding sufficient nourishment soon fell a prey to famine, which, before long, was followed by a still more terrible scourge. This was a frightful epidemic produced by the multitudes of insects and the bodies of animals which were left unburied. Then to the bustle of a happy people succeeded the unbroken silence of a depopulated and deserted country. Our misfortunes in particular had become so great, that we wept no more for those of our number who had died. We carried the corpses of my sisters to the forest without shedding a tear. As we placed them in the hut my mother observed.

"'Happy they, whose misfortunes were thus cut short.' Instead of carrying my youngest brother to the forest, my mother buried him in our cottage itself, and then taking my hand set out with me on a weary journey along the banks of rivers, without casting a farewell glance to her native hills and fields."

Poor widow! Poor orphan! While endeavouring to escape, they were but going forward to meet fresh misfortunes.

CHAPTER VII.

SOME days had passed since Suema had described the famine by which her country was ravaged, when, at the request of the reverend mother, she continued as follows :—

"The change of place greatly benefited my unhappy mother. She regained her fortitude; and at the distance of a three days' journey we built a hut, and commenced to dig up the ground. A neighbour was kind enough to lend us two sacks of mtama—one for sowing, the other for food till the harvest. Though I cannot say that complete happiness once again entered our little cottage, yet, my mother became more tranquillized, and I was delighted to perceive that she no longer wept. But, alas, our peace was not of long duration. The year was bad, and the harvest completely failed. Our creditor, pressed by necessity, came to reclaim the mtama which he had so kindly lent us. Greatly embarrassed at this demand, my mother threw herself at his feet, entreating him to grant her a little delay. But the reprieve she obtained was altogether insufficient.

"Without losing courage, my good mother had recourse to her ordinary industry, and especially to her skill in clay work. Neither by night nor by day did she desist from her work in which I assisted her as much as lay in my power. However, you must know that works of this kind are of little value in certain countries. Thus, notwithstanding all our exertions, we were unable to pay the quarter of our debt, at the expiration of the term fixed by our creditor.

"Returning to seek his debt again, and finding that we were still unable to pay, he departed uttering threats, which caused us much pain. To crown our misfortunes, an Arabian caravan passed by us very soon after. Who is there who does not know how dangerous for the weak is the approach of a caravan? Wicked neighbours are accustomed to steal their children and to sell them to the Arabs, either for salt or for beads. Creditors also profit of these occasions to enforce the payment of their debts. When the latter are unable to pay, their slaves or their children are seized upon. It even happens that often they themselves are reduced to slavery. There is not, after all, anything very astonishing in this apparently strange conduct, for the avarice of those who do not love the true God can neither be curbed or restrained within any limits whatsoever. We heard soon that the caravan had stopped at some short distance from our cottage. On every side spread the greatest uneasiness. During the night the sobs of my mother awoke me several times. Fearing to increase her trouble, I did not dare to ask her the cause of her tears. But, in the morning, I was not long without perceiving that she had been oppressed during the night by some most extraordinary grief. Fancy what must have been my astonishment when I saw that her hair, in one night had become as white as milk! Poor mother! in her maternal anxiety she had foreseen the blow which was about to strike us. Her fears were realised. In the morning, with our creditor, came two old men of his tribe, and an Arab. Without asking leave, they entered the hut and said harshly to my mother. 'Mother of Suema, you have nothing to pay for my sacks of mtama: I will take your daughter in payment.' 'Bear witness,' said he then to the old men. Then turning to the Arab he said—' Well! it is agreed: 110 yards of American cloth for this little child!' The Arab took me by the hand, made me rise and walk about, examined my arms and feet, opened my mouth; and then, after some moments' reflection he replied, ' It is well—you can take the cloth.'

"I was sold! During all this time my mother seemed as if in a swoon. But when our inexorable creditor told her that he had seized me for his debt according to the legal usage of the country, she covered her face with her hands and wept; for her grief, till then pent up, burst forth in heart rending sobs, and when she saw the Arab leading me away she threw herself at his feet, and, in a voice which no language can express, supplicated him to take her also. ' I am not yet old,' said she, ' for my hair is white not from age, but from sorrow. I am yet strong enough to carry an elephant's tooth. Ah, for pity's sake do not separate me from my child—my sole consolation in the evils which weigh me down. Master, I entreat you, do not refuse me this one favour. Besides, I can content myself with very little food, and I know how to work earthenware. I would be useful to you as a slave, and I promise to work constantly. Do, my lord, my master, do bring me away with you. Pity an unfortunate mother who wishes not to be separated from her child!' These words coming from the inmost depths of my mother's heart softened the Arab. I think, however, that in consenting to attach both of us to his caravan, he was influenced less by my mother's tears than by the advantage he might gain from her labours in earthenware. Whatever was his motive, the decision tranquillized our agitated hearts."

So distressing a scene, in which maternal love manifests itself in the highest degree, proves that even among these abandoned tribes, whose character is susceptible of many Christian virtues, human nature is not altogether depraved. Is not this the place to recall to our memories the words in which the great Pope St. Gregory expressed his feelings when he saw the natives of Great Britain exposed for sale in the Roman market: "What a misfortune it is that such beautiful creatures are the slaves of the Devil." The noble pontiff vowed that he would save them, and he was faithful to his word.

CHAPTER VIII.

JOURNEY IN THE DESERT.

THE interest of the little community of Zanzibar, in the fate of Suema, increased more and more as her history progressed, and all eagerly desired to learn as quickly as possible the catastrophe; however, in order to recruit the child's strength the continuation of her narration was postponed for a few days, when Suema resumed her narration:

"Early the next day the caravan set out. The heavy burthen of an elephant's tusk was put upon my mother, while I had only to carry some pieces of cloth. The following is the manner in which the caravan travelled. Immediately after midnight some of the master's servants hasten on before the caravan, taking with them ropes and axes to construct huts; others, again, to draw water, carry pitchers, and besides, a large drum to collect the entire caravan. They are also provided with an antelope's horn, which is considered by them to be an infallible talisman against lions and all other wild animals. These they generally purchase at an exorbitant price, from the most famous magicians in the country. At day break the signal for departure is given, and immediately a man, protected by an enchanted flag, places himself at the head of the column. This is more generally the distinctive sign of some powerful native chieftain, who thus affords them a somewhat more substantial protection. Then come the slaves who carry the provisions, ivory, copal gum, and the clothes of their masters. The latter, accompanied by some faithful servants, brings up the rear. At mid-day the Arab prays for some moments, and every one rests for two or three hours. The march is then resumed, and kept up till the evening, when provisions are served out. Those in advance take great care to mark the way by covering with leaves and grass all the paths which lead off from the caravan's direct route. Towards evening they beat the drums to guide more securely those who follow in the rear. Arrived at the resting place for the night, the caravan finds the huts all ready. They are generally made with branches of trees and dry herbs. In the best one a bed is constructed with leaves and branches for the accommodation of the master. The rations, which have also been prepared beforehand, are then distributed. They generally consist either of a kind of pap thickened with meal, or of beans, to which roasted banana, bread or soft potatoes are often added. In order to husband the strength of those laden with wares, as well as to prevent desertion the conductors take good care to nourish, as well as possible, the slaves under their charge."

In this manner the Arabian caravans safely traverse thousands of leagues under the scorching tropical sun, and all to gain money at the expense of the life or liberty of unfortunate negroes. As the caravan, which is carrying Suema far away from her native land, moves on, pause for a moment, young Christians, to compare your lot with hers, ask yourselves what would you wish to be done for you, were you in her place.

CHAPTER IX.

FILIAL LOVE.

LET us re-enter the hall of the community where the missionaries, the nuns, and the children are collected—Suema is going to continue the history of her life.

"The two or three first days of the march passed over well enough. I had a natural love for walking, and, fortunately, my burthen was not very heavy, but such, however, was not the case with my poor mother; the first day, laden with an elephant's tusk, she walked at the head of the column. During the second day she dropped back to the middle; the third day it was with difficulty that she kept up with the rear of the caravan. Every now and then she left down her charge. Her difficult and painful breathing betrayed her fatigue, and each step showed the superhuman efforts she made to continue the journey. Every suffering of my mother that I could not aid pierced my heart like a dart. The following day the caravan had the misfortune to miss the streamlet it had followed till then, and every one was parched by a burning thirst. My mother, exhausted by fatigue, and succumbing under the weight of her burden, fell several times. Seeing that she was incapable of any longer carrying her heavy load, the master ordered a slave to carry the tooth she had dragged from the time she had joined the caravan. I was for a moment consoled, and even astonished, to behold these principles of humanity in an Arab. Cruel deception. What was my grief when I overheard in the evening this barbarous command given to the slave, whose duty it was to distribute the victuals. 'Suema's mother is no longer of any use. For the future do not give her any rations.' What tidings for a daughter who dearly loved her mother! By dissimulating, however, I managed to divide my rations with my mother. Unhappily, the ferocious Arab perceived my innocent ruse, and he beat me till the blood ran down. He then gave orders to serve out my allowance in his own presence, and that I should be watched as closely as possible. The following day my unhappy mother had nothing else to subsist upon but a few locusts, some leaves of matama, and a little red earth. What a situation for her unhappy daughter! In the evening I could not eat. I was ashamed to taste the good food which was offered to me. How could a child who saw her mother perishing with hunger dare to eat?

"But this feeling of tenderness and filial compassion was so badly interpreted by the inhuman Arab that he had me beaten again, and I was forced to swallow the food, watered by my tears, without having the consolation of sharing it with my wretched mother. The next day—oh, day of misfortune!—our caravan entered an immense plain which had just been burned, and the fire extended farther than one could see. No longer any traces of green herbs, nor of insects, nor of birds were to be seen. Nothing met the eye save a boundless sea of blackened earth. It was absolutely impossible for my mother to procure the slightest morsel of food, not even some red earth to fill her craving stomach. During this day I saw her fall several times, spent with fatigue, and loss of breath. It was but by the most superhuman efforts that she succeeded in arriving at the resting place for the night. At the serving out of the rations my ear was again rent by these inhuman words. 'Let some one,' said the master, drive this old woman from the encampment, and mind well that no one give her anything to eat : Whoever infringes this order shall be severely punished.' Then he cruelly added, 'To-morrow, Allah be praised, we shall be disencumbered of her—to-morrow, I hope, she shall leave us in peace; this is her last stage: she can do no more.' These words were accompanied by a ferocious laugh which explained its entire meaning.

"Can anyone describe the feelings by which my heart was agitated, while this barbarian gaily pronounced the sentence of death on the only person whom I loved passionately in this world—of my beloved mother who loved me so much, and who had sacrificed herself, that she ought not be separated from me at least in this world ? The words grief, anguish, despair, are too feeble to express the least of my sufferings. The sole thought of these torments makes me shudder, even at this present moment." Indeed, in truth, Suema suffocated by grief was obliged to cease. All the community were deeply moved at her emotion, and it was not till after a long interval that the poor orphan could continue her heart-rending story.

"In the night we slept under the canopy of heaven, for the fire had consumed all the herbs and bushes. It was a very desirable lot for me, at least, when I was enabled to rejoin my starving mother. As soon as I thought that everyone was asleep I glided like a serpent out of the camp. The darkness of the night, and the black colour of the plain, with that of my body, favoured my flight. I must, however, confess, that when but some few hundred feet from the resting place, I felt myself stricken by a great fear; as I was never accustomed to walk alone in a dark night; my blood curdled with dread. I was unable to proceed further; the love which I felt for my mother arose within me stronger than ever, and I shouted out aloud. 'What, ought not a daughter suffer for a beloved mother? Is it not better to die with her than to survive her?' These words gave me new courage, and I bravely pursued my way."

CHAPTER X.

MATERNAL LOVE.

LET us rejoin Suema, and follow the footsteps of this young heroine of filial piety.

"I walked as much as the darkness of night would permit me, in the route pursued by the caravan. I held my breath, listening attentively to catch the slightest noise. Soon I heard deep groans, by which I recognized my mother's voice, and knew she was not far distant. I ran towards her, crying out, 'Mother, console yourself, here's your child coming to comfort you.' She heard these words with sighs of love and of tenderness. When at length I had the happiness to discover her she folded me in her emaciated arms, placed my head on her knees, and I felt her tears falling down my cheeks. She rocked me as much as her shattered strength would allow, as formerly she rocked my brother. Then she sang in a very low tone, as is the custom at our funerals.

"'Suema, my child, why did you not die with your sisters? I would at least have had your tomb, a happiness which none could take from me. Happy is the mother who can breathe her last, weeping over the graves of her children. The graves of your brothers and sisters are far away, and you are about to be eternally separated from me. But I am no longer able to follow you, nor to return to the graves of your sisters. Oh! alas! where are you going, unfortunate child? Death is not as bitter as slavery. Who shall longer care and tend you in distress? The cold morning dew and the wintry rain alone must wash the orphan's head. The naked earth is to be her bed. The grave is her home, the only place where she can rest her aching limbs.'

"Thus wailed my mother, sobbing all the while according to our customs, and my heart was almost bursting. The tears no longer flowed from my eyes, for I felt as if choked with grief. I thought my throat was filled with hot coals. My breast was rent with sorrow. However, the soft rocking and plaintive voice of my mother, joined to the fatigue of a long day's journey, soon lulled me to sleep, and at daybreak I felt that some one was clasping me very tightly. I awoke, and perceived I was folded still in my mother's arms. Then I heard the noise of men who were evidently looking for me. They approached and saw us, and summoned their companions. They surrounded us on all sides. The Arab, rolling his eyes in a most terrible way, first seized my hand and sought to drag me away by force. But my mother clasped me so closely that the cruel man, though he dragged us along the ground, could not succeed in separating us. Trembling with rage, he yelled out in a hoarse voice 'beat off this cursed old hag; cover her with stripes.'

"Immediately a shower of blows descended upon my unhappy mother, who, notwithstanding all her sufferings, pressed me closely to her side. 'Strike me, beat me away as long as you like, she faintly said. Strike, but I will die before you separate me from my last child.'

"The master heard her, but he would not even leave this last consolation to my dying mother. 'Strike,' said he, and 'beat the little girl severely.' The pain caused by the blows which followed drew the most piercing cries from me. At length, my mother's strength failed, her arms were relaxed, and I was seized and carried off. Making one last effort, my mother threw herself on her knees, and sorrowfully stretched forth her hands towards me. A moment after I saw her fall back, without doubt suffocated by grief."

Suema's affliction was great. Nevertheless, there still remains at the bottom of the cup some drops more bitter than all the others, and these has Suema yet to drink.

CHAPTER XI.

THE LAST SEPARATION.

SUEMA was already treated and regarded by the missionaries, the nuns, and her little companions, with the deepest compassion and the liveliest tenderness. She was looked upon as almost a martyr. These sentiments became more marked as the end of her story was well known to all. On the request of the superiors she related it as follows:—

"I struggled as much as I could in the arms of the slave who bore me away when I tried to obtain a last look at my mother. Soon they got tired of carrying me, and tried to urge me on with blows. At each step I tried to return to my mother, or weighed down by blows and suffering I fell to the earth. Wearied by my resistance, the master ordered a slave to take me up again and carry me to the encampment. He obeyed: scarcely had we arrived when the caravan set out. We soon came to the summit of a hill. I looked behind, and in the centre of the scorched plain, for the last time, saw my mother, her arms still extended towards me. But by what new torments was my heart racked when I saw, wheeling around her head, a countless flock of ravens impatiently awaiting the moment of her death to tear the flesh from off her bones. No one could possibly even conceive what I suffered at that moment. More dead than alive, it was, however, necessary for me to proceed. If I slackened my pace in the least I was mercilessly beaten. I shall pass over our journey from the spot whence last I saw my mother to Quiloa, which is a town situated on the coast. I only know that during this long journey from shedding so many tears, my eyes became so swollen, that I was in dread of becoming blind. Still they beat me to make me walk on. But all their cruelties were without effect, for so weighed down was I by my afflictions, that I was not able even to keep myself upright. 'Master, said the slave to the leader of the caravan, 'what's the use o' carrying this skeleton any farther? You see the child is no longer fit for anything, but to be torn in pieces by the ravens. 'I cannot leave her here,' he replied, 'as I bought her for my master. If I leave her behind I lose the piastre (4s. 6d.), which you are aware I get for each.' The man who carried me was furious, and he did all in his power to get rid of me. At every halting place he threw me as heavily as he could to the ground. Passing under the trees and through thorny brakes he never failed to flay my back with the branches.

"But, besides all this, what was really worse, this inhuman conduct excited not only the laughter but the approbation of the wretched companions of my captivity. We spent a few days at Quiloa: they were for me but a short respite in my miseries. There no one ill-treated me. I lay down to rest in the darkest corner of the hut. The water flowed almost within my reach, and permitted me to quench at liberty my burning thirst. It was by that stream that my life was preserved. What pleasure did it not afford me as I cooled my parched tongue with its limpid waters! To every thing else I was completely indifferent. I scarcely knew where I was, and I had but a faint remembrance of my long sufferings. All the time from the moment that I was taken away from my mother, till our arrival in Quiloa, appeared to me like a horrible dream. I even thought that this dream would have an end, that everything which surrounded me should fade away, and that I would awake one day beside my bereaved mother, in the little hut where we were so sad, but happy in comparison with our present lot."

As you said, poor child, all that was but a hideous vision. The reality which awaited you was sadder still.

CHAPTER XII.

THE VOYAGE.

AFTER having suffered, during a long journey, in the scorching heat of the tropic regions, all the fatigues, all the ill treatments, all the privations, every bodily, every internal torture, Suema had now to undergo all the sufferings of a voyage—a voyage which was to be made with its accompanying hardships.

Let us hear the dear child describe it with her ordinary candour and precision.—

"While deluded by these illusions, and in a state of mind by which I barely knew that I still lived, one morning I was hurriedly carried on board a small vessel bound for Zanzibar. All the slaves, who like me had just been embarked, commenced to tremble and bewail their misfortunes in the strongest manner. 'Ah,' said they, 'we are all lost. We are going to

Zanzibar, where white men live that eat up the poor negroes.'

"Though I was generally indifferent to all that passed around me, yet I could not remain any longer in the position I then occupied, and I began to wish for death. But my sufferings were redoubled in the vessel. We were so pressed that it was not only impossible to stir, but even to breathe. The heat and thirst became insupportable, and to crown all, a strong gale began to blow which completed our miseries. In the night we were frozen by the cold air of the open sea, and covered every now and then by the foam which was dashed over us by the violence of the wind. On the following day, each of us received a little fresh water, and some mania root.

"In this manner did we pass six long days, and six longer nights. Cold, thirst, sea-sickness, the sudden transition from the highest degree of heat to an icy coldness, impossibility of resting our head even for a moment, from want of room; in fine, all these sufferings united, made me regret for the first time, our journey across the desert. But I took courage, my life soon changed—we were already in sight of Zanzibar. The triangular sail was now swelled by a strong wind, and we quickly arrived before the capital. Two cannon shots shook the vessel, the sail was taken down, and the anchor dropped. I heard my companions in misery admire the walled city—the white city. Every other moment they were either lost in admiration, or plunged in the deepest fear. As for me, my eyes were closed to the light, and what passed before me, passed as if a thick mist. I only lived in the hope that once on firm earth again, some one would give me a little water to allay my burning thirst. Oh! how cruel a torment is thirst. I do not remember how we were landed, nor how long we remained at the courthouse. The sight of this immense crowd of Negroes carrying heavy burdens on their shoulders, their cries had made me so giddy that I could no longer take notice of the thousand objects which passed before my eyes. Besides, it was becoming dark already."

CHAPTER XIII.

SUEMA BURIED ALIVE.

"WHEN we arrived at the slave depot, which is a large stone house, it was already night. There I saw the conductor of the caravan, whom I had before looked upon as the most powerful person in the world, demean himself humbly before another Arab, who appeared as if reproaching him, in a language which I did not understand. I think he must have been scolding him on my account, for he pointed several times at me with his finger.

"Then in another language which resembles that of my country he ordered me to get up. I made many efforts to do so, but without success. 'This slave is useless, said this new personage; it is a great loss to me. Six yards of cloth, her transport by sea and land, and the custom house duties, at least there are 55 piasters (one pound) lost. Conductor, henceforth commit no such follies.'

"Then turning towards two stalwart negroes he added, 'Khamis and Marzoule, put this skeleton into a mat, and carry it to the cemetery. It's useless to nourish her longer, for she can't be saved.' As soon as this order was given it was executed. I was at once folded in an old mat by the two slaves who took good care to tie it up well with cords of cocoa. They then hung the mat on a long piece of wood, and lifting it to their shoulders carried me far away from the depot. I was so enveloped by the mat that I could no longer see anything, but the noise of the crowd told me that I was being carried through the streets of the city. To the noise of the large city succeeded the rustling of branches, by which I knew that we were passing through a brake. At last they stopped, and threw me on the ground. I felt that they were scraping up the sand, then I felt that I was being buried alive. The layer of sand which covered me was so thin that I could hear the footsteps of the negroes as they hurried away. The deepest silence ensued—a most horrible fear seized upon my whole being. I had undergone many sufferings before that moment. From my earliest years my life had been but one of sorrows. However, the mere thought of death was a source of inexhaustible terror to me. I then made a violent attempt to disengage myself from the mat but without success, and it was but with the greatest difficulty that I could raise my head over the sand to prevent being suffocated. At the same time I commenced to shout out as loudly as I could. But my feeble voice was lost in the silence of the night. Two or three times I thought I heard footsteps passing quite near me. I shouted still louder. But my voice instead of bringing me succour, frightened travellers whom I plainly heard going away.

"A deep silence again ensued. All at once the brake was agitated near the spot where I was buried. Hope again came. Suddenly a pack of yelping jackals surrounded me. My blood froze with terror. My cries and the desperate efforts I made kept them away for some time. But little by little they encouraged one another, and I heard their baying come nearer and nearer. At last they disinterred the extremity of my body, and I felt them biting at my feet. I cried out once more and then fainted off."

We ask the question again. Is it possible—can it be possible—that there are on the surface of the globe beings, who bear the name of men, so barbarous, so inhuman, so unnatural as to treat thus unfortunate human beings? Yes, there are, alas, but too many— we must not cease to repeat it to all Christians—too many there are too forgetful of what they owe to Christianity and to their brethren still doomed to the hardships of slavery.

CHAPTER XIV.

SUEMA DELIVERED.

PROVIDENCE had not forgotten the poor orphan. Suema had drunk the last drop of her bitter chalice. He who brought her to the portals of the grave, and will conduct her back, already comes to her succour. Hear in what manner He came.

"When my senses had returned, I found myself in a chamber with white partitions. I was lying in a good bed covered with a white blanket. Two persons with white faces, such as I had never before seen were standing at the head of the bed, and were watching attentively every movement I made. They were dressed in white and black. They were you, dear mothers; yes, you, the true daughters of Mary, who guarded me so tenderly, and devoutly. Seeing their black habits, I thought for a moment that I was dead, and in the land of the Peponi (spirits). My first thought was for my mother.

"'Where is my mother?' I enquired several times of the sisters whom I took for spirits. 'Be quiet,' replied one of them, 'your mother will be here soon.' I was then presented with a most delicious draught which I eagerly swallowed, and then fell back asleep.

"I will now tell you what passed during the loss of my senses while I was surrounded by the howling jackals.

"M. N., a young creole of Bourbon, not being able to sleep that night, took into his head the fortunate whim of hunting jackals. Armed with his gun he was directed towards the cemetery by the howling of the jackals. Instead of flying as the other passengers he bravely attacked the animals, at that very moment ready to tear me into pieces, and put them to flight; then seeing before him a bundle which was stirring a little, the young man naturally wished to know what it was. He stopped, opened the cords, unfolded the matting, discovered a warm body, lifted me upon his shoulders, and carried me to the Catholic Mission House, where I was joyfully received by the good mothers. My deliverer was loaded with the warmest congratulations for the charitable deed he had the happiness of performing. From that moment I was happy."

Let us partake of the happiness of Suema. Let us admire the designs which Providence so wonderfully carried out in the person of this little child. Saved from the greatest perils, and brought by the longest and most painful way into the motherly bosom of the church.

CHAPTER XV.

SUEMA'S CONFESSION.

WHEN Suema had finished the recital of the external dangers she had undergone, she wished, at the request of the superior, to lay bare the inmost workings of her heart to her young companions. She acquitted herself of the task with her ordinary candour.

"I would have ended my narration, dear sisters, where my misfortunes ceased. However, since our mother wishes, I will reveal to you a fact, at least to me very serious, and which is intimately linked to my unhappy state of life. We all learn here, happily for ourselves, the consoling truths of religion, and the duties which it imposes on us. Each word of our Saviour has been for us new light, filling us with consolation. We, poor orphans, have found good mothers, who have made us know our real Father, the good God. We have been despised, persecuted, and illtreated. They have taught us to love those who despise, who persecute and illtreat us. They have ended by persuading us that our tears have brought down the benedictions of our good Jesus, who will crown us one day with a great glory if we are good Christians. Without father and without family, we have found both in this mission house, which, besides, shows the way to our true home where there are no more sufferings.

"All the truths I have been taught have given me the most ineffable consolation. My soul drank them in as I would formerly drink a glass of fresh water, while travelling across the sandy desert. But when one of the mothers explained to me the Lord's prayer, at these words—'and forgive us our offences as we forgive them who trespass against us'—I felt my soul revolting from that command. Everything else is good enough but that is insupportable. I could not contain my hatred against those who persecuted me—a hatred enraged with bitterness and sorrow. And going to the nun, I said to her, 'Mother, ought I, must I pardon the Arab who struck my dying mother? Oh, no, never shall I forgive my mother's assassin!'

"' My child,' replied the nun, ' our Lord, God as he is, suffered the greatest insults. He forgave them all; he even prayed for his executioners.'

"' But, mother, such a thing is utterly impossible : I think if I said yes, my heart would whisper, your pardon is not sincere.' The good nun embraced me and said, 'I pity you, my poor Snema, on account of the long and cruel sufferings that you had to endure, and on account of the obstacle you place in the way of your baptism, which would have crowned all your desires. It is a great loss, dear child; you have learned with such zeal your catechism, and here now you do not wish to lay aside that wicked hatred, as you would renounce Satan, his works, and his pomps. With this hatred, baptism is out of the question; but pray, my child. I will also pray for you, and with God's grace, your heart will relent.'

"I set myself to pray, and in the midst of my prayers I felt myself sometimes happy, and sometimes unhappy. In the day I thought I could sincerely say 'yes, I pardon with all my heart that cruel man.' But, the following night, I dreamt that I was assisting at the following scene which took place in the black desert :—I thought I was changed into a raven, that

E

the Arab lay drenched with his own blood in the middle of the plain, and that I tore him into pieces with my beak, beating my wings all the time. I related this dream to the nun; it brought the tears into her eyes. She said softly to me 'continue to pray dear child, God will have mercy on you.'

"The day of my baptism was already fixed. It came at length, but the sacrament which would make me a Christian had to be deferred, because my disposition was scarcely changed."

The forgiveness of injuries is the greatest miracle of Christianity. In this circumstance, the conduct of the Arab, the filial tenderness of Suema, the fiery nature of African people, explains Suema's repugnance. But God's grace is stronger than Nature.

CHAPTER XVI.

HEROISM OF SUEMA.

HER Baptism deferred, Suema was unhappier than ever.—But Providence, which had protected her in so many dangers, did not wish that this dear child should be lost at the very mouth of the harbour. In a separate wing of the house is a room where sick people of every race and religion are gratuitously received, and attended with the most delicate care. "One morning," continued Suema, "some one came to tell the superioress that several Arabs, wounded in a fight with some English cruisers, had just been carried into the room. It was my turn to help the Sisters of the infirmary. I hastened to prepare everything necessary. The hot water, the basin, sponge, lint, all was ready in a few moments. Carrying all these, I entered the hall with some of the Sisters.—Oh, wonder of wonders!—The first person who met my eyes was our old leader of the caravan, who had struck my dying mother. He was in a terrible state. His head cleft with a sabre cut, his chest bloody, and deeply marked by several bayonet wounds, made such an impression on me, that I let the things I had in my hands fall to the ground, nor could I help exclaiming, My God! it is the Arab!!!

"The reverend mother turned towards me, and said in a voice full of kindness, 'Suema, my child, your misfortunes merit their reward, and now behold, in his mercy, our Lord has vouchsafed to you an occasion to perform an action which will gain for you an inestimable prize. Happy those who have the generosity to do good for evil; God will one day remember it. A little courage, child, and the victory is yours. Suema, you must dress the wounds of this man."

"My eyes met those of the reverend mother, and I obeyed the order which was given, trembling in every limb the whole time. I took the basin, and commenced to wash the cuts. The first attempt cost me much— Oh, how much! Besides the disgust I naturally felt, my lips were ready at that moment to curse my enemy. I was internally glad that he was wounded. But little by little, with God's aid, I overcame myself, and those bad thoughts were succeeded by the deepest pity. I was myself astonished at the change which had taken place within me; and it was not until then that I experienced all the delights of Christian charity. After dressing the unfortunate man, I retired secretly to the nun's oratory, and there, prostrate before the altar of the Blessed Virgin, I sobbed aloud these words, 'O Mary, my mother, have pity on that wretched man whom you gave me courage and grace to forgive; yes, I pardon him sincerely—truly.'

"At these words I felt warm tear drops falling on my head. I turned round and beheld the nun who first taught me the precepts of the Catholic Religion. She had heard me pronounce the words of forgiveness, and it was she who shed over me the tears of love and delight, blessing God for the grace of my conversion. She was so happy that she folded me to her heart, as my mother did, when I saw her for the last time. This was on Sunday. Towards evening I was given a white robe, and half an hour before benediction the pastor's flock was increased by one more lamb, and the Catholic family had another child. In baptizing me, the Holy Church added to my name of Suema that of Madeleine, which is a thousand times dearer to me than the first.

"I spent the remainder of the day in thanking God,

who by his mysterious and admirable ways, guided me safely to the light of the gospel. I said to myself every moment, 'What have I done that I should be preferred to so many millions of infidels who never shall have the same happiness?'

"Penetrated by this thought, I wished to testify my gratitude to our Good Master, and was not a little embarrassed to know what I could do most agreeable to his Sacred Heart.

"I heard then, as if a voice saying to me interiorly, 'Madeleine, live as a good Christian, and then do all you can to obtain the conversion of your countrymen.' 'Yes, yes, my God,' I cried, 'I take that resolution in Thy presence; all my life I will work for that end. I will pray to Thee every day in order that Thou, in Thine infinite mercy, mayest have pity on the infidels of Oriental Africa, and that Thou mayest send them missionaries to show them the way to heaven.' Madeleine kept her word.

Such is the authentic history of Suema, and thus has it been sent from Zanzibar, by the Rev. Fr. Horner, Apostolical Missionary of the Congregation of the Holy Ghost, and of the Immaculate Heart of Mary, Superior of the Mission in Zanzibar.

CONCLUSION.

*I*N conclusion of this moving narration, the superior wrote: "Oh that you could, Monseigneur, see with your own eyes the children bought by you, and those whom you have inspired with sentiments of Christian charity! Your heart would be happy at the sight of these little creatures, who do not yet know how to speak French, but who do not fail to recite every day their beads in the *Souahili* language, known by God, for the benefactors who bought them from slavery. They pray for them every day in this life, and hereafter will bless them throughout all eternity." Then he adds, "How heartrending it is to the missionary to be unable to rescue so many souls, for whom, in consideration of a little money, the gate of heaven would be opened.—What a sad thought it is to think that for 50 francs (£2), a child from 6 to 7 years old could be ransomed; that even that trifle is not to be had, for it is but too often spent on foolish and even dangerous frivolities. What an amount of good could be done with more resources." Young Christian ladies, to whom we have been inspired to especially address this tale, if you only hearken to the voice of your heart, we are sure that there is not one among you who would not wish, according to her resources, to console the venerable Missionary, and to share in the ransom and conversion of so many millions of *poor blacks*, the most unhappy, and the most abandoned beings in the world.

They stretch forth to you their suppliant hands and entreat you, while exposed for sale in the market of Zanzibar, "White lady, buy us, and we shall be happy." And you also, dear children, you shall be happy, happy even now by the very thought of the good you will do, happy in the future by the certainty of the recompense which is promised to you by Him, who says, "Amen, I say unto you, as long as you did it unto one of these my least brethren, ye did it unto me." (St. Matthew xxxv. 40.)

After reading the history of Suema, if any person young or old, be desirous of doing some good, let them know that in the market of Zanzibar a little boy or girl, from 4 to 8 years old, ordinarily costs from 40 to 50 francs (£1 12s 6d to £2.) This sum, whether furnished by one or more persons, will be received with the liveliest gratitude by the Rev. Father Procurator General of the Congregation of the Holy Ghost and the Immaculate Heart of Mary, for the Mission at Zanzibar, 30, Rue L'homond à Paris; or by Mgr. Gaume, 16, Rue de Sèveràs Paris; or at the French College, Blackrock, Dublin.

www.ingramcontent.com/pod-product-compliance
Lightning Source LLC
Chambersburg PA
CBHW020151170426
43199CB00010B/995